LOS ALAMITOS SCHOOL

Donated by:

Kelli Dinger

Squirrels

Squirrels

by Joe Van Wormer

E. P. DUTTON   NEW YORK

LIBRARY OF CONGRESS CATALOGING IN PUBLICATION DATA

Van Wormer, Joe.   Squirrels.

SUMMARY: Describes the physical characteristics,
habits, and natural environment of various members
of the squirrel family.
1. Sciuridae—Juvenile literature.
[1. Sciuridae.   2. Squirrels]   I. Title.
QL737.R68V35   1978   599'.3232   78-5804   ISBN: 0-525-39860-0

Published in the United States by E. P. Dutton, a Division
of Sequoia-Elsevier Publishing Company, Inc., New York

Published simultaneously in Canada by Clarke,
Irwin & Company Limited, Toronto and Vancouver

Editor: Ann Troy   Designer: Riki Levinson
Printed in the U.S.A.   First Edition   10 9 8 7 6 5 4 3 2 1

To Dick and Esther Wray
who have been with me all the way.

There are over a thousand kinds of squirrels in the world. A tiny one in Africa is no bigger than a mouse. A giant bushy-tailed tree squirrel in Southeast Asia is as large as a house cat.

A western gray squirrel

It is easy to see why the squirrel's name means "shade tail."

The squirrels we most often see in parks and woods are covered with gray or reddish brown fur and weigh from 1 to 3 pounds. Bushy tails wave behind them when they run, or curl over their backs when they are still. The tail forms half of the squirrels' 15½- to 24-inch length.

It is the tail that gave squirrels their name. A long time ago, Greeks named the animal *skiouros*. From this came

2

A yellow-bellied marmot from Oregon

the scientific genus name *Sciurus,* which means "shade tail," and the common name "squirrel."

In America there are woodchucks, marmots, and prairie dogs, which scientists put in the same family with squirrels. They are all much bigger than our other squirrels and do not have large bushy tails. They live in underground dens. They are not as common as bushy-tailed squirrels.

3

Marmots usually eat sitting up.

Woodchucks and marmots are much alike. Woodchucks live in the eastern United States, most of Canada, and part of Alaska. Marmots live in the western United States, including Alaska, and in western Canada. Their color varies from dark reddish brown to orange brown to cool gray.

Marmots hold food with their front feet.

They may weigh from 4 to 14 pounds and are the largest members of the squirrel family in North America. They eat various grasses, farm crops, melons, and apples. For this reason farmers do not like them very much. In late summer they eat more than at any other time and get very fat.

5

When the weather turns cold, marmots crawl into their dens and curl up into balls in a warm, grass-lined nest. They go into a deep sleep called *hibernation* for 4 or 5 months or even longer, depending on the climate. In this way they safely live through the times when food is scarce. During hibernation they breathe very slowly. Their hearts beat less than usual, and their bodies grow quite cold. They live on their own fat through the winter.

A yellow-bellied marmot in front of its rock pile home

Young black-tailed prairie dogs at the entrance to their underground Texas home

Prairie dogs live in the western prairies. They are called *dogs* because they often make a barking sound. They are yellow gray and about twice the size of a gray squirrel. They have short legs and short tails tipped with white or black. They live near one another in what are called *prairie dog towns.*

8

A prairie dog daintily nibbles a tender blade of grass.

Prairie dogs are grass and weed eaters. Sometimes when grasshoppers are plentiful, prairie dogs feast on them. Prairie dogs do not hibernate during the winter, nor do they store food. They stay in their dens when the weather is bad and do not eat. But on warm days they come out in the sun and nibble on grass left over from the summer.

9

Among the squirrels which look more like the squirrels we know are ground squirrels (including some called rock squirrels), chipmunks, tree squirrels, and flying squirrels. Ground squirrels and chipmunks live on the ground, have underground burrows, and feed mostly on flowers, seeds, plants, and insects. They can climb trees and bushes when they want to.

All tree squirrels have beautiful bushy tails. They live and nest in trees: sometimes in hollows, but often in high leafy nests they build themselves. They also spend a lot of time on the ground searching for food.

Flying squirrels don't really fly. They glide. Unlike all other squirrels, they feed at night and sleep during the day.

In the spring, a southwestern Colorado rock squirrel climbs a tree to feed on tender new buds.

Ground squirrels are found mostly west of the Mississippi River. They are often called *gophers* or *picket pin gophers* because of their habit of sitting up straight or standing up on their hind legs to look around to see if danger is present. However, they are not gophers. Gophers are small rodents that stay underground most of the time and are seldom seen.

In some places, ground squirrels are called picket pin gophers.

California ground squirrels have bushy tails similar to those of tree squirrels.

If a ground squirrel sees something it thinks is dangerous, it sounds a shrill, whistlelike warning cry. Then it may run to its den. Before disappearing underground, it usually turns around and pops its head out for another look.

14

Some ground squirrels, like this Mexican ground squirrel from the Rio Grande River area, have spots or stripes.

Except for California ground squirrels, Franklin's ground squirrels, and rock squirrels, ground squirrels do not have bushy "squirrel" tails. Some are plain colored. Others have special markings.

To cool itself, a California ground squirrel stretches flat against moist earth.

Ground squirrels spend most of their lives asleep. They hibernate in the winter, when the weather is cold. In the summer, when it gets very hot, they stay in their cool underground burrows and take month-long or longer naps. When awake, they spend most of their time gathering

16

A young Townsend's ground squirrel eating. Note its short tail.

food. What they don't eat, they carry into their burrows and store for future use. All ground squirrels have pouches in their cheeks. They can carry a lot of grain there. A captured Richardson's ground squirrel had 269 grains of oats in its cheek pouches.

Sometimes there are too many ground squirrels. Their big appetites and underground homes do much damage to farms. Often farmers and ranchers must destroy many of these squirrels to keep their crops from being ruined.

Ground squirrels are born in the spring. Some species that live in warmer areas may have two litters a year. There may be from two to thirteen babies in a single litter, but the average is six or seven. They are born hairless, with their eyes closed. They don't look much like squirrels then. They stay in the burrow for a month or so while the mother feeds them with her milk. Their fur grows and their muscles develop. After a time their eyes open, and before long they are peeking curiously out the den entrance at a strange big world. They gradually move outside and within about a month leave home for good.

A female Townsend's ground squirrel stands guard in front of her den.

A white-tailed antelope ground squirrel searches for seeds on the desert floor.

Antelope ground squirrels are busy little brownish fellows that live in the dry plains, deserts, and lower mountain slopes of the western United States. They are often mistakenly called chipmunks because they are about the same size as chipmunks and have white stripes on their backs. But they do not have stripes on their noses like chipmunks. Their small, flattened, white-backed tails are carried over their backs. They live in underground bur-

rows which they dig, but they also live in old burrows dug by other desert animals.

Antelope ground squirrels are busy hunting food every day except during stretches of cold weather. Then they stay inside and eat stored seeds. They escape summer's midday heat the same way. In addition to seeds, they are fond of grasshoppers and other insects. They can climb cacti and other prickly desert plants without getting stuck.

21

The handsome golden-mantled ground squirrel is also often confused with a chipmunk. It is a little larger than a chipmunk and has beautiful golden brown fur on its head and shoulders. Its face is more rounded than the chipmunk's. It does not have white and dark stripes on its face, but it does have them on either side of its back.

This squirrel lives in the higher mountains of the West. It hibernates from September to April.

In campgrounds and parks of the West, golden-mantled ground squirrels have learned to accept food from visitors, sometimes from their fingers. They may even sit on your knee while they eat peanuts.

BUT THEY NEVER BECOME TAME ENOUGH TO HANDLE. NO SQUIRREL OF ANY KIND SHOULD EVER BE PICKED UP, HELD, OR TEASED. THEY WILL BITE AND BITE HARD.

The golden-mantled ground squirrel is a native of our western mountains.

Two golden-mantled ground squirrels

All squirrels have four sharp front teeth, two upper and two lower. They can cut through the shell of the hardest nut. The teeth wear against each other as the squirrel chews. This keeps them sharp. These teeth never stop growing, so they never wear out.

24   Golden-mantled ground squirrels are great fun to watch.

A golden-mantled squirrel with cheek pouches full of nuts

They scamper about searching for food or playing. On hot days they may lie flat with their stomachs against a rock to keep cool.

They carry food to their dens in their cheek pouches. When the cheek pouches are full, the animal's face looks very fat.

25

A chipmunk drinks from a forest pool.

Chipmunks are found in all the states except Alaska and Hawaii. However, several central and southeastern states do not have very many. Most of central Canada has chipmunks, and Mexico has a few.

Chipmunks are easy to recognize, for they all have dark and light stripes on their rather sharp-pointed faces. A full-grown chipmunk is small, about the right size to hold in

Like other squirrels, the chipmunk usually sits up to eat and holds food with its front feet.

your hand. BUT DON'T TRY IT! Chipmunks also bite.

They eat nuts, fruits, berries, seeds, and many insects. They climb bushes and sometimes trees. They also have large cheek pouches, and they store large quantities of food in their underground burrows. Chipmunks may not actually hibernate, but they do take long naps during bad weather.

27

The gray squirrel is the bushy-tailed tree squirrel we see most often. It is found in parks, where it has learned that people and peanuts go together. It is the common squirrel of the woods and a favorite target of hunters. During the early days of our country, there were millions of gray squirrels in the forests. They became much-needed food for the pioneers.

An eastern gray squirrel in the moss-festooned trees of a Florida
swamp

An albino eastern gray squirrel

Gray squirrels are not always gray. Sometimes they are white. These are called *albinos*. They have white fur and pink eyes, and ordinarily do not live long in the wild. Their white coloration makes it easy for enemies to see

A melanistic eastern fox squirrel. A melanistic gray squirrel would look much the same.

them. Sometimes they are black. Black squirrels have an excess of melanin, a dark pigment, in their skins and are called *melanistic* squirrels.

31

Gray squirrels are found in the eastern half of the United States and in Oregon, Washington, and California in the West. They are about 18 inches long. Half of their length is the big bushy tail which makes them look very graceful when bounding along a high branch or along the ground. It gives them balance in jumping, climbing, running, and making quick turns. If the animal should fall, the tail acts as a parachute. On sunny days it makes shade. In cold weather it is wrapped around the squirrel's body to keep it warm.

A western gray squirrel

A threatened gray squirrel streaks for safety to the nearest tree.

This squirrel, like others, has large dark eyes, placed so that it can see in almost every direction without moving its head very much.

This is important, for squirrels are hunted by many other animals. Hawks, foxes, coyotes, snakes, skunks, bob-cats, raccoons, and badgers are always after them for food. A squirrel must be alert and fast if it wants to stay alive.

Right: The gray squirrel, like most other rodents, has large eyes.

When threatened by some enemy, a gray squirrel runs to the nearest tree and scampers up the trunk. Once it is in the tree, it may hide by flattening against the trunk and staying on the side opposite an enemy. Or it may climb high in the tree and lie on top of a branch so it cannot be seen from below. It may also run out to the tip of a branch, jump to another tree, and escape by going from tree to tree.

Sharp claws enable gray squirrels to run straight up or down tree trunks.

A gray squirrel gathers nuts even when it isn't hungry. It buries them one at a time.

Gray squirrels feed on different kinds of nuts, especially acorns and hickory nuts. In one week, a grown squirrel will eat its own weight in nuts. It finds the nuts with its keen sense of smell, which also tells it when nuts have kernels.

Gray squirrels spend a lot of time gathering nuts. Some are eaten. Some are buried, one at a time, and later may be dug up for food. The nuts that are missed often grow into needed trees. Gray squirrels also like wild fruit and berries, insects, and occasionally, eggs from a handy bird's

A gray squirrel's nest

nest. They do not have cheek pouches for carrying food, as do ground squirrels.

Gray squirrels hide in their tree nests to escape from enemies, to sleep at night, or during bad weather. Their nests look like an armful of dead leaves lodged in the upper branches. Baby squirrels, usually four to six at a time, are born in these nests. They are born pink and naked, with their eyes and ears shut. They weigh about ½ ounce or about as much as a fifty-cent piece. Captive gray squirrels have lived as long as fifteen years.

Left: A western gray squirrel attacks an intruder. *Above*: Only occasionally will battlers actually get hold of each other. The one on top has its eyes closed, probably to protect them.

Gray squirrels do not hibernate, but when there's a lot of snow, or when it's wet or windy, they stay in the nest. They do not store food in their nests, so when they get hungry, they go down to the ground and hunt for the nuts they have buried.

They guard their food discoveries, and if another squirrel or a bird comes too close, they chase it away.

Fox squirrels look like gray squirrels but are a little larger and a different color. Generally, the upper body is reddish gray, and the underparts are rusty yellow or orange. In the Southeast, fox squirrels may be black or dark brown with white noses and ears. The gray squirrel is mostly gray on top and white underneath. Fox squirrels are found in the eastern two-thirds of the country. Some were moved to the West Coast and became the start of a population of wild fox squirrels.

Fox squirrels do about the same things that gray squirrels do and often live in the same patch of woods. They also eat the same things. They both like to carry their food to a stump or some other high perch, so that while they eat, they can look over the land and see any approaching danger.

Florida fox squirrels are black or dark brown with white noses and ears.

Kaibab squirrels are shy. Those that are seen run along the ground at high speeds or sit in the tops of 60-foot ponderosa pines.

Possibly the most beautiful of all our squirrels are the tree dwellers of the high ponderosa pine forests of Colorado, Arizona, and New Mexico. These are the tassel-eared squirrels, named for their long ears which grow 2-inch winter tufts of blackish hairs that stick straight up. All other squirrels have short ears.

There are two species of these large squirrels, Abert's and Kaibab. The Abert's is the more plentiful and lives

south of the Grand Canyon and east of the Colorado River. It is gray and brown underneath. Its large bushy tail is grayish on top and white on the bottom.

There are not many Kaibab squirrels. They live in a small area on the north side of the Grand Canyon. They are similar in color to the Abert's squirrel except that they are black underneath and their plumed tails are flashy white.

A red squirrel

The red squirrel chatters, barks, and sputters. It is the noisiest of all the squirrels. Rusty red in color, these are the smallest of the tree squirrels. They are about 12 inches long and are found in most North American forests. Their tails, though not as showy as those of other tree squirrels, keep them warm in winter, and on course as they race up and down trees with amazing speed.

The Douglas squirrel is a western red squirrel.

The red squirrel needs all the speed and agility it can find to escape its enemies, especially the tree-climbing pine marten. Sometimes, in its frantic efforts to escape, a red squirrel will jump as far as 8 feet from one tree to another.

Red squirrels eat a great variety of food, including buds, bark, seeds, fruits, nuts, and mushrooms. They like meat and sometimes prey on young birds and birds' eggs.

This squirrel prefers a hollow tree nest and often lives in old woodpecker holes. When there are no hollow trees, the squirrel may build a leaf nest. A litter of five or six babies is born in the spring.

Red squirrels do not hibernate during the winter.

The Douglas is a western variety of the red squirrel and is about the same size. It lives in evergreen forests in the Pacific Coast states and British Columbia in Canada.

A red squirrel feeding on pine seeds

A southern flying squirrel. Note the flat tail, essential to the animal's control when gliding.

One of our most interesting squirrels is seldom seen. It sleeps during the day, eats and travels at night. This is the flying squirrel, which doesn't really fly at all. It glides on folds of loose skin between its wrists and ankles. When it wants to travel, it scampers to a high spot in a tree, takes aim, and jumps. It spreads its front and hind legs, and stretches the loose gliding skin. On this "wing" it glides down through the air for long distances.

A southern flying squirrel gliding

These little squirrels are very good at landing exactly where they want to. Glides of 20 to 30 feet are common, but some are as long as 160 feet. Just before landing, the squirrel flicks its tail upward and thrusts its feet down to make a slowing parachute of loose skin. It turns its body upward and lands with a soft thump on all four feet against the trunk of its target tree.

There are two species of flying squirrels in North America. The southern flying squirrel is the smaller, about 9 inches long, of which half is tail. This species lives in the eastern half of the United States. The northern flying squirrel is a bit larger. It is found over most of Canada, part of Alaska, on the Pacific coast, and in the northern Rocky Mountains.

A southern flying squirrel rests on the side of an oak tree.

Feeding time. These tiny squirrels favor hickory nuts. They cut through the hard shells with their sharp teeth.

Both kinds of flying squirrels look alike. On top they have very soft brownish fur. Underneath they are white. Their rounded heads and pert noses are topped by large black eyes which enable them to see well during their normal nighttime wanderings.

Southern flying squirrels may raise two families a year. When born, they are the size of an inch-long piece of lead

Two little flying squirrels eating side by side

pencil. The usual litter is two to six babies. They nest in all kinds of places—hollow trees, attics, old farm buildings, birdhouses, and even in old gray squirrels' nests.

They eat the same things that tree squirrels do and store much food for winter use. Often they are active at night in the same trees their larger tree squirrel relatives run about in during the day.

Flying squirrels seem to enjoy company. Sometimes as many as fifteen or twenty live in the same nest.

They do not hibernate but stay in their nests during cold, windy, or wet weather. They may sleep on their sides or backs, or curled up like a ball. They even sleep while hanging on to a wall by their toenails, either head up or head down.

Flying squirrels and all squirrels are important to other wildlife. By burying nuts which sometimes grow into trees, they help to maintain the ecological balance of nature.

A curious flying squirrel peeks out of its den.

INDEX